crochet your own
holly jolly garland

Kati Gálusz

becker&mayer! books

Brimming with creative inspiration, how-to projects, and useful information to enrich your everyday life, Quarto Knows is a favorite destination for those pursuing their interests and passions. Visit our site and dig deeper with our books into your area of interest: Quarto Creates, Quarto Cooks, Quarto Homes, Quarto Lives, Quarto Drives, Quarto Explores, Quarto Gifts, or Quarto Kids.

Published in 2021 by becker&mayer! books, an imprint of The Quarto Group, 11120 NE 33rd Place, Suite 201, Bellevue, WA 98004 USA.
www.QuartoKnows.com

This book is part of the *Crochet in a Day: Crochet Your Own Holly Jolly Garland* kit and is not to be sold separately.

becker&mayer! books titles are also available at discount for retail, wholesale, promotional, and bulk purchase. For details, contact the Special Sales Manager by email at specialsales@quarto.com or by mail at The Quarto Group, Attn: Special Sales Manager, 100 Cummings Center Suite 265D, Beverly, MA 01915 USA.

21 22 23 24 25   5 4 3 2 1

ISBN: 978-0-7603-6945-6

Library of Congress Cataloging-in-Publication Data available upon request.

Author: Katalin Gálusz
Photography: Chris Burrows

Printed, manufactured, and assembled in Shenzhen, China, 05/21.

Distributed by:
Quarto UK, The Old Brewery
6 Blundell Street, London N7 9BH, UK
Allen & Unwin
30 Centre Rd, Scoresby VIC 3179, AUS

Image credits: All stock photographs and design elements © Shutterstock

#339911

Contents

About This Kit

This kit contains the tools and materials you will need to make a yard-long holly garland: yarn in red, green and brown; an E/4 (3.5mm) crochet hook; and a yarn needle.

How to Read the Instructions

Every line starts with the round/row number in bold, and ends with the stitch count in parentheses.

Instructions in square brackets must be repeated the specified number of times before continuing with the remaining instructions of the round or row (if any).

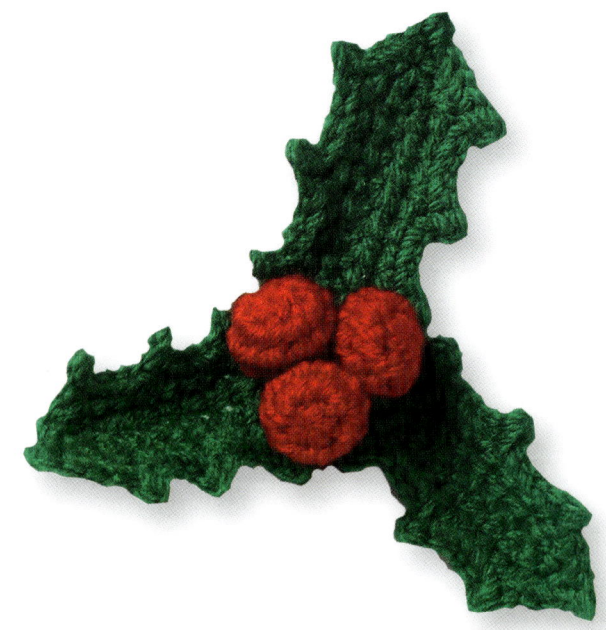

Abbreviation Chart

CH	**CHAIN OR CHAINS**
INC	**INCREASE**
INVDEC	**INVISIBLE DECREASE**
P	**POINT**
RND	**ROUND**
SC	**SINGLE CROCHET (US)** **DOUBLE CROCHET (UK)**
SL ST	**SLIP STITCH**
ST	**STITCH OR STITCHES**
YO	**YARN OVER**

Notes on Tools and Materials

YARN

The garland in this book was designed with worsted weight yarn, but if you want to make more garlands, you can use any yarn thickness: as long as you stick to it throughout, and choose a matching hook, your project will turn out just as fine, only smaller or bigger than the original.

HOOK SIZE AND GAUGE

Exact gauge is not important in this project, as long as you work tight enough to create a fabric that's fairly stiff and doesn't gape visibly. To achieve this, you will need a hook size smaller than recommended on the yarn's label. The sample garland was crocheted with E/4 (3.5mm) hook, but this is only a guideline; feel free to experiment to find what best suits your crocheting style.

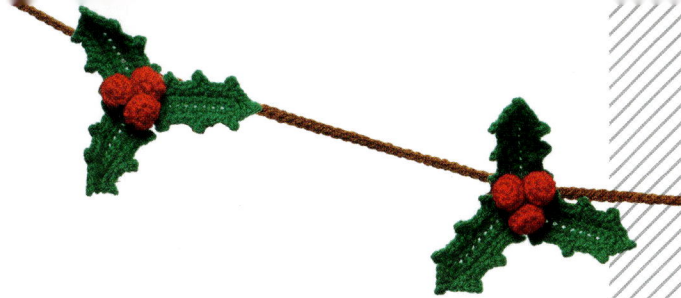

NEEDLES

Blunt tapestry needles are usually recommended for sewing knit and crochet pieces, but for decorative projects I prefer a chenille needle or yarn needle because its sharper point can pierce through yarn if necessary for a neat join.

STITCH MARKER

Because most of the parts are worked in a continuous spiral without joining, you will need a stitch marker to keep track of your rounds. There are special split-ring markers for crochet, but safety pins or paper clips work just as well.

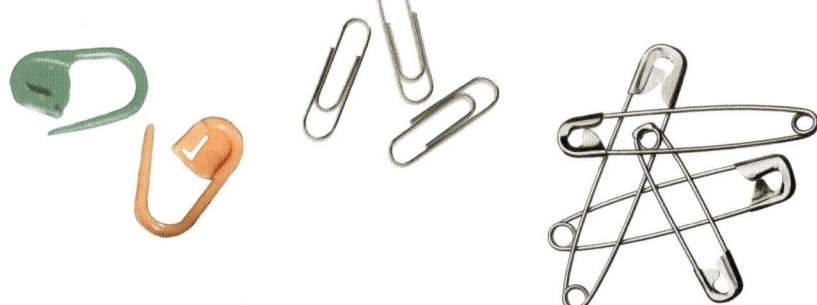

Crochet Stitches and Techniques

This chapter contains a short primer on the techniques you will need to create the garland, but if you are new to crochet, I suggest you to practice the basics before starting the actual project. Many yarn shops offer classes, or you can look up video tutorials online.

SLIPKNOT

Use this to begin a chain. Make a loop on your yarn a few inches from the end. *(Fig. A)* Insert your hook through the loop and grab the yarn end connected to the skein. Pull the strand through the loop, then tighten the knot. *(Fig. B)*

YARN OVER (YO)

Wrap the yarn around your hook from back to front.

CHAIN (CH)

Make a slipknot first, unless you are in the middle of a piece and already have a loop on your hook. YO, and pull yarn through the loop on hook. Repeat as many times as required. *(Fig. C)*

The loop on the hook doesn't count as chain, so omit it if you are checking the stitch count.

WORKING INTO A CHAIN

Usually, you have to skip the ch nearest to the hook and work your first st in the 2nd or 3rd ch from hook (the pattern will always specify this). *(Fig. D)*

When you look at a row of chains, the front side will look like a series of tiny Vs, and the back will have a single ridge of loops. For the neatest look, insert your hook into the back ridge rather than the front V.

WORKING INTO STITCHES

Every stitch has two strands in a small V shape on top. Insert your hook under both sides of the V unless otherwise specified.

WORKING IN FRONT/BACK LOOP ONLY (FLO/BLO)

When you look at the V on top of the stitch, the strand closest to you is called the front loop and the strand farthest from you is called the back loop. If you need to work in front loop only, insert your hook under the closest loop only. If you need to work in back loop only, insert your hook under the farthest loop only. *(Fig. E)*

SINGLE CROCHET (SC)

Insert your hook into the st or ch, YO and draw up a loop (pull yarn through st or ch). You will have 2 loops on your hook. YO and pull yarn through both loops on hook. *(Fig. F)*

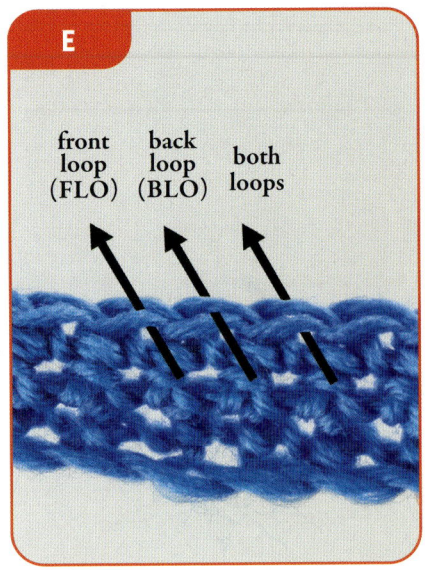

INCREASE (INC)

In this pattern, inc always means single-crochet increase: work 2 sc in the same st. *(Fig. G)*

INVISIBLE DECREASE (INVDEC)

While this stitch can be replaced by the more common sc2tog (single-crochet-2-together), it produces a much smoother look, so it's really worth learning for amigurumi.

Insert your hook in the front loop only of the st (no YO here!) Swing the hook slightly downward so you can insert it into the front loop of the next st. YO and draw up a loop through both front loops. YO and pull through the 2 loops on hook.

SLIP STITCH (SL ST)

Insert your hook into the st or ch, YO and pull yarn through both the st or ch and the loop on hook. Be careful to keep the stitch loose: the V on top should be the same size as the top of other stitches.

POINT (P)

Sc 1, ch 2 *(Fig. H)* and sl st in the 2nd ch from loop *(Fig. I)*, sc 1 into the same st as the previous sc *(Fig. J)*.

FASTEN OFF

To finish your piece, cut the yarn 3-4 inches from your hook (or more, if you will need the yarn end for sewing), and pull the end through the last loop on the hook.

WEAVE IN YARN ENDS

In amigurumi, many yarn ends are luckily on the inside of the piece, so we don't have to deal with them. But there is the end left after closing up a body part, as well as the leftover yarn after sewing together pieces. To secure these, stitch through the body several times to catch it in the stuffing. Then pull the yarn tight and cut it right in front of the crochet fabric – the tension will pull it back inside the body.

WORKING IN CONTINUOUS ROUNDS

Amigurumi is mostly crocheted in rounds, starting with a small circle of stitches and progressing in a continuous spiral without turning or joining. To keep track of the beginnings/ends of your rounds, attach a stitch marker in the first st of the round, moving it to the next round when you start it. *(Fig. K)*

K

MAGIC RING

The magic ring is a nice technique to start working in the round, because it will create a small circle of stitches with no gap in the center.

Make a circle of the yarn. Insert your hook through this ring *(Fig. L)*, YO and draw up a loop *(Fig. M)*, then ch 1. Work the first round of stitches over both the ring and the free yarn end, then pull on the free end to close the ring.

RIGHT & WRONG SIDE

If you are working in rounds without turning, your project will have a right and a wrong side. The right side is the side facing you while you work; this should be the outside of your piece. On the right side, individual stitches resemble small Vs *(Fig. N)*. On the wrong side, they are like an upside down V with a horizontal bar on top *(Fig. O)*.

It is quite usual for your work to start curling up in the wrong direction. Stop after the first two or three rounds to check, and if necessary turn the piece right side out.

L

Materials

- 35 YARDS (30M) RED WORSTED WEIGHT YARN
- 55 YARDS (50M) GREEN WORSTED WEIGHT YARN
- 15 YARDS (17M) BROWN WORSTED WEIGHT YARN
- E/4 (3.5MM) CROCHET HOOK
- YARN NEEDLE

Finished size: 1 yard (0.9m) long garland

Instructions

LEAVES (MAKE 15)

RND 1: With green yarn, make a slip knot and ch 10. Starting from the the 2nd ch from hook, inc *(Fig. A)*, sc 7, then work 3 sc in the last ch. Continue working into the other side of the starting chain (at the base of the stitches) *(Fig. B)*, sc 8 (20)

RND 2: Inc, [sc, P, sc] 3 times, P *(Fig. C)*, [sc, P, sc] 3 times (9 points made)
Sl st 2 *(Fig. D)*, then fasten off leaving 10" tails on five leaves and 3" on
the rest. Weave in all short ends. *(Fig. E)*

E

Arrange one leaf with a long tail and two without tail so that they touch at the base. Thread the yarn end into the needle and sew the leaves together. *(Fig. F)* Weave in the yarn end.

Repeat for the remaining leaves, making a total of 5 clusters.

OPTIONAL: STIFFENING

If your leaves won't stay flat, you can starch them to stop them from curling. You can either use a commercial fabric stiffener, or make a simple sugar solution which works just as well. Combine ½ cup of sugar and ½ cup of water in a small saucepan. Heat it until the sugar is completely dissolved, then let it cool down. Wet the leaf clusters with plain water, then dunk them into the sugar syrup. Squeeze out the excess syrup, then blot the leaves with a clean towel to remove as much liquid as possible. Lay the leaves flat on a plastic wrap covered surface and let them dry completely.

F

BERRIES (MAKE 15)

RND 1: With red yarn, make a magic loop, sc 6 and pull the ring tight (6) *(Fig. G)*

RND 2: Inc 6 (12)

RND 3: Sc in each st (12) *(Fig. H)*

Make sure the berry is turned right side out. Stuff the end from the magic loop inside the piece. Since the berries are tiny, there is no need to use actual stuffing, they will hold their shape well enough anyway.

RND 4: Invdec 6 (6)

Fasten off leaving a short end.

Thread the yarn end in a needle. Push the needle through under the front loop of the next st, from inside out. *(Fig. I)* Repeat in each st around the hole, then pull the yarn end to close the gap. Push the needle through the center, and bring it out between the stitches near the top of the berry. *(Fig. J)* Pull the yarn end tight and cut it off as close to the crochet fabric as possible.

If the berries are flattened by all the handling, gently roll them between your fingers to return them to their original round shape.

I

Thread a 10" length of red yarn into the needle and stitch through the bottom of 3 berries, then through the first berry again. *(Fig. K)* Tighten the yarn to pull the berries together *(Fig. L)*, then secure the group by tying the two yarn ends together. Do not cut off the ends!

Repeat this for the remaining berries, making a total of 5 clusters.

K

CORD

With brown, make a slip knot. Ch 7, sl st in the 7th ch from hook (this will make a small loop for hanging the garland) *(Fig. M)*, then ch until the cord measures 1 yard. Ch 7 more. Sl st in the 7th ch from hook to make the other hanging loop, then continue toward the beginning of the chain: sl st in each ch. *(Fig. N)* When you reach back to the first hanging loop, fasten off and weave in yarn ends.

ASSEMBLY

Stitch the yarn ends from the berries through the leaf clusters. *(Fig. O)* Distribute the holly pieces evenly along the cord and (still using the yarn ends from the berries) tie them to the cord. *(Fig. P)* Then thread each end into the needle again, stitch through the leaves, bring out the yarn end near the top of a berry, pull it tight and cut off right in front of the crochet fabric.

p

Great job! Enjoy your Holly Garland!

#CrochetInADay

About the Author

KATI GÁLUSZ discovered the world of amigurumi when she wanted to make a unique gift for a toy-collector friend. What started as a quick fling has grown into the love of a lifetime, allowing her to combine her need for creativity with her two main interests, animals and great books and movies. After lavishing her creations on her long-suffering family and friends, she started to sell them on Etsy and share her crochet patterns on Ravelry. When she is not crocheting, she can be usually found with a book in her hand, surrounded by her dogs in her home near Budapest, Hungary.

ALSO
AVAILABLE

crochet your own
reindeer ornaments

crochet your own
merry and bright baubles

crochet your own
candy cane ornaments

crochet your own
spooky skull garland

crochet your own
festive pumpkin